# DEGAS

## LIFE AND WORKS

# DEGAS

## LIFE AND WORKS

**VIRGINIA SPATE**

SOURCEBOOKS, INC.®
NAPERVILLE, ILLINOIS

# Introduction

Edgar Degas was born in Paris in 1832. His was a rich and cultivated upper-middle-class family that shared the attitudes of its class: a secure sense of position, belief in controlled, well-bred behaviour, and an unquestioning acceptance of the good life of the Parisian social élite. Early in his career, however, Degas came to accept the fundamental principles of Realism: truth to the visible world, combined with an understanding that such truth was shaped by personal experience. This meant that he would see the world with his own eyes, not the eyes of others. It also meant that he would paint the world he knew: modern life in Paris, as experienced by someone of his class. He painted portraits of his well-to-do family and friends, as well as scenes of their work and recreation, but his privileged status also gave him access to lower-class life: to the backstage world of ballet dancers, to the hidden, claustrophobic spaces of the brothel, and to the vulgar attractions of *café-concerts*. He depicted such subjects with a curious detachment, refusing any moral judgement, but using his art to reveal the 'modern beauty' that they contained.

Realism required the artist to look at human beings as if they were objects, and, in this sense, it was an ideal form of art for Degas. Perhaps because of the death of his mother

*Self portrait* 1885

when he was just 13 years old, Degas found relations with others difficult. He expressed this best in a 1890 letter to an old friend, Evariste de Valernes (*see page 33*), in which he apologized for having often been brutal in their discussions on art:

I was or I seemed hard with everyone by a sort of impulse towards brutality which came to me from my doubts and my ill-temper. I felt myself so badly formed, so badly equipped, so soft, while it seemed to me that my ideas on art were so true. I sulked against everyone and against myself.

Degas had a malicious wit; he was touchy, obstinate and often prejudiced. But he also inspired lifelong friendships. He never married, and has been accused of being a misogynist, although, again, he had long friendships with women. Relatively few of his paintings contain both men and women, and they tend to be isolated from one another, or even antagonistic. Except in paintings of parents and children, few of his figures touch or even look at one another in any intimate way. Most of his works represent women – usually working-class women. He would obsessively repeat the same pose as if somehow trying to possess it. But perhaps it was his detachment from others that gave his depiction of women a certain dignity, however degraded their existence, and however ungainly the poses that he depicted. He did not, like Renoir, mold them into the desirable shapes of erotic fantasy, but showed them as plain, even ugly, active beings. His paintings thus invite the spectator to see these women as individuals.

### The 1850s and 1860s: From the Classical to the Contemporary

Degas first studied drawing when he attended a prestigious school in Paris. When he left, he continued to draw and to copy works in the Louvre. In 1855, he visited the revered classicist painter Jean-Auguste-Dominique Ingres (1780–1867), who advised him to, 'Make copies, young man, many copies, and you will become a good artist.' Ingres would have meant copies of classical sculpture, and of works by artists who followed the classical tradition. Degas did indeed 'make copies,' but his art was to be far from classical.

It was unusual for someone of Degas's class to consider becoming an artist, but he was nonetheless encouraged by his father, who supported him financially. He could have developed a respectable career by following the traditional route of academic art: years of study in the École des Beaux-Arts (School of Fine Arts), where teaching was based on intensive study of the human figure – which students had to learn to idealize according to the example of the approved masters of the past. Such a training was directed to the creation of works of 'high art,' the most important of which were paintings of religious and historical subjects intended to elevate the mind and the emotions through their beauty and subject matter. Academic theory did not value paintings of contemporary life, although there was a considerable market for them if they were sentimentalized or moralized. Portraiture was well regarded if the sitter were idealized. Success in the great annual exhibition – the Paris Salon – was crucial in such a career.

But Degas did not follow this course. After only a few months in the School of Fine Arts, he went to Italy, where he spent three years studying the Old Masters through sketches and copies. When he returned to France in 1859, he began painting formal portraits and history paintings as if planning a conventional career. Nevertheless, in the early 1860s he met with Édouard Manet (1832–83) and other young artists who were interested in painting modern subjects, and, by the second half of the decade, he seems to have decided to become a Realist painter of contemporary life. It is not known what made him take this decision, but his history paintings (for example, the *Spartan Girls challenging* the Boys; see page 24) reveal an almost unconscious attraction to visual truth that made it impossible for him to give them the idealization, harmony, and 'finish' that academic art required.

Painters had been painting contemporary life since the 1840s, but, fearing and despising the changes brought by modern capitalism, they usually depicted the timeless world of the peasant. However, from the late 1850s onwards, there was intense debate about a new kind of Realism that would express the characteristics of modern city life. It was believed that the city's dynamism, its scale, and its crowds had created a new form of consciousness: alienation and a detached but ceaseless fascination in all that the city offered. Novelists characterized the 'modern body' as casual, informal, shaped by work. Degas began to depict such a body quite early (see pages 28, 33, 37, and 40). He almost certainly read Charles Baudelaire's essay 'The Painter of Modern Life' (1862), in which the writer called for a new style of painting to represent modern dynamism – a rapid, shorthand style whereby a broken line or patch of color could evoke the wholeness of the body (see, for instance, the outstretched arm of the singer in Café-Concert at the Ambassadeurs; page 62). Degas was to paint many of the subjects that Baudelaire described as characteristically modern: horse-races; theatre's world of illusion; the world of fashionable women; and the demi-monde of courtesans and prostitutes. Baudelaire valued the artificial, ultra-civilized life of modern Paris, however corrupt, over what he saw as the meaninglessness of nature. Degas shared this obsession, once saying to another artist, 'for you natural life is essential, for me artificial life.'

After 1865, Degas devoted himself entirely to paintings of contemporary life. However, although these paintings look completely different from the Old Masters he had studied, his mode of working remained traditional: he always worked in the studio, relying on his prodigious memory and on sketches of his motif. His paintings might appear like the immediate reaction to something seen, but they were, in fact, meticulously prepared by means of drawings and studies or by the multiple repetition of a theme. 'No art,' he wrote, 'was ever less spontaneous than mine. What I do is the result of thought and of the study of the Old Masters.'

**The 1870s to the Mid-1880s: The Ethnographer of Paris**

Degas remained in Paris during the terrible events of 1870–71, when the Prussians besieged the city, and the Paris Commune was suppressed amid terrible massacres and the destruction of many fine buildings. Perhaps the threat to Paris – the 'city of light' and of shadowy, hidden depths – made Degas more conscious of it than he had been previously, for he now devoted himself to representing its multiple life more intensively than ever. By 1872 he had begun his first paintings of ballet dancers rehearsing their meticulous and arduous art (*see page 44*), and had returned to his paintings of the racetrack. After visiting relatives in New Orleans in 1872–3, he painted a family portrait (*see page 51*), in the context of a rarely depicted aspect of modern life: the business world.

Separation from Paris may also have intensified Degas's awareness of the city's unique qualities, for on his return, he enlarged his modern-life subject matter: his rare depictions of middle-class women now included family portraits and images of the American painter Mary Cassatt at the Louvre (*see page 89*); he also painted gentlemen backstage and at the races, a financier at the Stock Exchange, and a writer in his study (*see pages 81*). But the vast majority of his Parisian subjects were of working-class women – laundresses, singers in the *café-concerts*, prostitutes, and, above all, ballet dancers.

Degas saw his world through the assumptions of his class. He depicted ladies with strong but refined features (*see pages 20, 48, and 112*), but he painted – and probably *saw* – working-class women with coarse, ill-formed faces (*see pages 62 and 71*). He was consciously influenced by the theories that held that the shape of heads revealed inherited personality traits. Many now believed that these theories were scientifically validated by the theory of evolution, according to which humans had evolved from animals, and more civilized humans from primitive ones. The Parisian upper classes therefore felt justified in considering themselves a higher level of being than the more animal-like working class. But, at the same time, they feared that such animality was a sign of the inevitable degeneration of civilization. In 1874, the writer Edmond de Goncourt described Degas as:

A sickly hypochondriac with such delicate eyes that he fears losing his sight and for this reason is sensitive and aware of the reverse character of things. He is the man I have seen up to now who has best caught the atmosphere of modern life and the soul of the present.

The 'reverse character of things' probably meant those hidden aspects of modern social life that could be revealed only by the intense observation of surface appearances. Other writers described Degas's depictions of different Parisian types as a form of 'scientific realism' or as 'ethnographic,' while the critic and novelist J. K. Huysmans wrote that his study of modern life was characterized by an 'analytical insight at once subtle and cruel.'

Degas displayed extraordinary inventiveness in this period: he was influenced by the graphic shorthand of the caricaturist Honoré Daumier (1808–79), and by Japanese prints, which suggested entirely new ways of seeing the world. To intensify the vibrancy of color and the impression of spontaneity, he experimented with new techniques, notably with dazzling combinations of monotype and pastel. Such works were unlikely to have been accepted by the Salon: they lacked 'finish' and depicted 'vulgar' subjects unredeemed by any moralizing. Moreover, his works tended to be small and so required intimate viewing. It was for such reasons that Degas joined with a group of artists – including Claude Monet, Pierre-Auguste Renoir, Berthe Morisot, Camille Pissarro, Paul Cézanne, and Alfred Sisley – to found an exhibition that was independent of the official Salon. At the first exhibition in 1874, the press named the group 'Impressionist,' but Degas never accepted the label, for he scorned both the practice of open-air painting and the immediate reaction to the motif to which his colleagues attached so much importance. But he did share with them the ideal of truth to personal vision, as well as that of capturing a 'moment' in time (such as the moment when light catches a dancer as she turns in space; *see page 72*), and they exhibited together, or squabbled about exhibiting together, until 1886.

After his father's death in 1874, Degas became burdened with family debts, so he needed to sell, and sell fast, despite his own desire to keep his works and to continue working on them for years. Like Monet and Cézanne, he saw painting as continuous research into the world of sight – and into the processes that transformed the raw material of sight into the intense concentrated world of art.

**The Mid-1880s to the Early 1900s: A More Abstract Art of Observation**

Degas's Realism had always had a tendency towards abstraction; it was never illusionistic – materials, for example, are always emphatically paint; this paint may suggest the visual effect of silk or of muslin, but it does not imitate them. But from the mid-1880s, this tendency became more pronounced: there are larger, more expressive masses of color, and the textures of paint or pastel are more emphatic. Instead of wide spaces full of visual incident, Degas now depicted enclosed, even claustrophobic spaces filled with larger bodies seen close up. This sense of enclosure was echoed in Degas's own life when he retreated into his studio; he did not exhibit in any group exhibitions after 1886 and, since he had paid off his debts and his work was in demand at good prices, he could afford to work primarily for himself. Symptomatic of this retreat into an interior space is his fascination with a new theme: nude women in corners of rooms; women tending to their bodies, grooming themselves; women crouching to sponge themselves or to comb their long hair; women stretching to get out of a bath or to dry themselves. They are observed with an obsessive intensity in all their intimate actions.

Degas also continued his equally obsessive exploration of the multiple, disciplined poses of the ballet dancers. Here, too, he tended to bring the figures closer to the foreground plane; the dancers are no longer individual, and there are only the most summary indications of the room. He concentrated on the infinite malleability of these bodies, their insistent self-presentation, the maintenance of pose even in intense weariness.

Later in life, Degas worked increasingly in pastel, achieving an extraordinary variety of effects. Since the early 1870s, he suffered from poor eyesight, particularly in bright light. By the early 1890s, he could scarcely see to read or write. But in 1890 he went on a joyful expedition through the countryside, and could see the landscape sufficiently clearly to re-create wonderful images in monotype and pastel (see page 119). It is impossible to know how much was observation, and how much the internalized memory of what the hands could create. Pastel, charcoal, and monotypes were media whose movements he could feel in his hands, those hands that were so accustomed to their own disciplined movements that he could perhaps rely on their 'memory' of the relationship between sight and form on paper – just as the dancers could rely on the deeply internalized shaping of their bodies: the necessary stretch, tension, leap across space. Degas had also been modelling in wax from the late 1860s onwards (see page 116), and this, too, was a means by which the hands could shape movement. Perhaps such modes of creation explain why Renoir could say: 'Degas painted his best things when he could no longer see.'

Degas now concentrated on what had always fascinated him: the process of creating form from inert matter. One needs to consider why this process should have been so closely associated with the bodies of women – of women preparing their bodies to be seen, washing, combing their hair, examining themselves in mirrors, rehearsing, adjusting their clothes, trying on hats. In 'The Painter of Modern Life', Baudelaire had written that the essence of modernity lay in its artificiality; art was significant not because it imitated nature, but because it created something more intense, more concentrated, more human. In this sense, a courtesan who transformed her body through clothes and cosmetics made her body into a work of art. The entire effort of the ballet dancers was to make their bodies into art. Degas's lifelong, concentrated attention to the movements of the human body, his disciplined rehearsal of the effect of each element of form, and his constant repetition of themes were directed to the same end.

Degas was the most acute observer of the mysterious otherness of the human body. But his art was not a matter of recording what he saw, but of searching out the forms with which he could express how he perceived his world. Through his consistent struggle to create such form, he created an intense, personal world, a world that can absorb the spectator into its being as if it were alive.

# The Early Years

## THE 1850S AND 1860S

*Roman Beggarwoman* 1857

39 x 29¼ in

Oil on canvas

Birmingham Museums and Art Gallery, Birmingham

Degas painted this work when he was in Italy studying the art of the past, as was believed necessary for any artist who aspired to a successful career as a figure-painter. Besides copying the Old Masters, many artists painted what they saw as picturesque Italian beggars and peasants. Usually such works were prettified, but here Degas observes the woman with almost pitiless realism, minutely describing the motley pattern of worn clothes, and every detail of her wrinkled face and veined hands. Yet he also makes the figure monumental, and, through his refusal to sentimentalize, he gives her the dignity of human presence, however humble.

***Family Portrait, also called The Bellelli Family*** 1858–67

78 x 97½ in

Oil on canvas

Musée d'Orsay, Paris


Degas's largest painting depicts the family of his aunt,
who had married the Baron Gennaro Bellelli. The psychological
tensions within the family are expressed through two clashing
styles. His aunt is posed with the grandeur of a seventeenth-
century aristocratic portrait; her expression is self-absorbed,
disdainful. Her husband is painted more sketchily, and his
casually slumped body is almost pushed into the corner of the
room, sharply divided from his family. One daughter is enclosed
within the dark silhouette of her mother, and the childish pose
of the other provides the only hint of spontaneous life in the
elegantly claustrophobic room.

Degas painted the work for the Paris Salon, probably as a grand
gesture to establish his reputation. He would not have intended
to display marital disharmony in a formal portrait, but his acute
sense of the expressive relationships between bodies makes
the formality of the group achingly revealing.

***Spartan Girls challenging the Boys*** c.1860–2

45½ x 60½ in

Oil on canvas

National Gallery, London

This was Degas's first attempt to create a major history painting with a classical subject. It shows the young men and women of the most warlike state of ancient Greece exercising naked or partially naked to prepare their bodies for war or for bearing sons for future wars. Degas followed academic practice by preparing the painting with drawings of the individual bodies, and compositional studies to work out the clear geometric space and arrangement of the figures – whose clear contours are illuminated by the steady light that characterized most classicist art. But Degas probably intended to make something very modern of the classical, for the bodies are not idealized: the boys have the gawky angularity of adolescents, and their features are coarse, while the girls do not have the seductively soft flesh characteristic of contemporary academic art. Degas's depiction of women as physically active beings was very unusual. The expressive use of empty space between males and females was to become a characteristic of his art.

*Semiramis constructing Babylon* c.1860–2

58¹⁄₂ x 100¹⁄₂ in

Oil on canvas

Musée d'Orsay, Paris

Degas did not finish this history painting, or the *Spartan Girls*, for exhibition in the Salon, but he kept them all his life and displayed them proudly, never suggesting that they had been superseded by his paintings of contemporary life.

While he was working on the *Semiramis*, Degas was also painting pictures of racehorses that show how vividly he could depict movement (*see page 28*), so one must assume that he intended to freeze the Babylonian queen, her attendants, and the horses into rigid immobility. Perhaps he was trying to imagine the grandeur and dignity of an archaic past uncluttered by the materialism that was expressed in his contemporaries' archaeologically correct reconstructions of the ancient world. He studied 'primitive' sources – Assyrian sculpture, archaic Greek art, the paintings of fifteenth-century Italy – to create an alternative world of dreamlike calm.

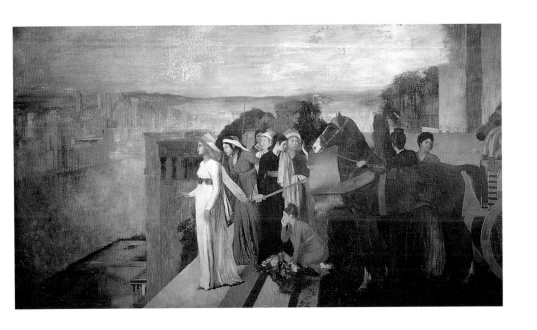

***At the Races: The Start*** c.1861–2

12½ x 18 in

Oil on canvas

Fogg Art Museum, Harvard University, Cambridge, Massachusetts

When Degas and Manet later disputed as to who had painted
contemporary life first, Degas claimed priority for his paintings of
horse-racing. These works mark the beginning of his lifelong
fascination with the representation of movement. At this time,
races were often held in open country, without elaborate stands
and with only small crowds, so Degas's paintings on this theme
are his most sustained exploration of figures in landscape – as
remembered in the studio. Here he gives a subtle rendering of
the sun and shadows cast by a stormy sky with a wonderfully
delicate vision of a distant town. In the foreground, he wittily
contrasts the slouched jockeys in their brilliant silks with the
elegance of the high-stepping horses.

**Self-portrait with Evariste de Valernes** c.1865

45¼ x 34¾ in

Oil on canvas

Musée d'Orsay, Paris

Degas was probably inspired by Renaissance double portraits. He depicts himself and his friend as elegant gentlemen, but his rigid body and the curious gesture of his hand make him seem ill-at-ease and melancholic in contrast to de Valernes's more relaxed pose and expression.

Degas originally wore a top hat but painted it out quite casually, scrubbing on creamy and silvery colors to suggest an impressionistic cityscape of domes and colonnades; in a similarly casual way, he juxtaposes one finished hand with a mere outline. Degas kept the painting all his life, probably as the record of a friendship, so he did not need to 'finish' it, but this lack of finish also reveals his tendency to reveal the processes of creation in all their rawness.

*Interior* c.1868–69

31½ x 45¼ in

Oil on canvas

Philadelphia Museum of Art, Philadelphia


This is one of Degas's most disturbing paintings. It may have
been inspired by Émile Zola's novel *Thérèse Raquin* (1867), in
which two lovers who have killed the woman's husband are
divided by their horrified memory of the killing. Degas does not,
however, illustrate the story, and thus lures one into exploring the
work more actively than one would if he had made the story more
explicit: Why is the man blocking the door so threateningly? Why
is the woman with her shift slipping off her shoulder turned away?
Is there significance in the brilliantly lit objects on the table, in the
chaste and narrow white bed, in the discarded corset? The pretty
wallpaper, the gilded frames, the smudgy mirror, even the warm
lamplight give an indefinable intensity to the threat of the man
and his dark shadow at the door.

*Carriage at the Races* c.1869

14 x 21½ in

Oil on canvas

Museum of Fine Arts, Boston, Massachusetts

This painting is a fairly descriptive and tender family scene showing a gentleman – probably Degas's friend Paul Valpinçon – his wife, the wet-nurse, and bulldog all gazing at the sleeping baby. It is one of the first works to display Degas's interest in Japanese woodblock prints, as seen in the the dark linear skeleton of the carriage, cut by the frame and silhouetted against the flat green plane of grass, as well as the witty cut-out shapes of horses and riders. Japanese prints offered alternatives to Western perspective space and to tonal modeling in ways that helped French painters express the newness and immediacy of modern life.

**The Orchestra of the Opéra** c.1870

20¼ x 17½ in

Oil on canvas

Musée d'Orsay, Paris

This group portrait contains Degas's first representation of ballet dancers – a subject that he was to paint more than any other. It depicts Degas's friend the bassoonist Desiré Dilhau and other musicians at work in the orchestra pit, and thus conforms to the idea that the modern portrait should – in the words of the Realist writer Edmond Duranty – reveal a man's 'wealth, his class, his profession' and depict him in his environment (*see page 81*).

Again, there is dualism between male and female space: the men are individual beings engaged in creative activity; the women, headless fragments of bodies, made momentarily beautiful as the footlights catch the tulle skirts. The scroll of the double-bass projecting into the female space is aggressively phallic. At a time when only women of the lower classes could reveal their legs, the emphasis on the ballerinas' limbs would have lured the contemporary gentleman spectator to imagine the private recesses of the female body.

# A Painter of Modern Life

## THE 1870S TO THE MID-1880S

**The Dance Foyer at the Opéra on the Rue Peletier** 1872

12½ x 18 in

Oil on canvas

Musée d'Orsay, Paris

The life of the ballerinas of the Opéra was one of hard work and a precarious future. Most depictions of ballet dancers played on the public's assumption that such women were prepared to sell their sexual favors. But Degas chose to show the disciplined work that underlay the dancers' art – just as he drew attention to the way he created form. For example, he created visual ambiguities that lure one into questioning exactly what one sees: the mirror in the arched doorway reflects unseen dancers; the open door on the left shows a fragment of a dancer echoing the one in the foreground. The harmony of interweaving whites, pinks, and blacks is brought to a higher pitch by red accents – in the fan, the sashes, the practice bar – all summed up in Degas's own signature, as if to emphasize that this was his creation.

***Woman with an Oriental Vase*** 1872

29¼ x 21 in

Oil on canvas

Musée d'Orsay, Paris


It was conventional in nineteenth-century portraiture to associate women with flowers, but no other Realist painter allows them to dwarf the female subject in such a way. Only the clear light on her face and dress prevent her from being overwhelmed by the monstrous plant. This woman is hemmed into a corner of the room by the furniture and the huge vase, and her curiously flexed hand and her sideways gaze seem to embody her tension.

Degas never made his portraits of women – who were always friends or members of his family – conform to conventional notions of beauty. This woman's face – with its slightly twisted mouth and slightly skewed eyes – is plain, but it gives the spectator the sense that she is an individual being with her own inner life.

***The Cotton Exchange, New Orleans*** (originally exhibited
as ***Portraits in an Office, New Orleans***) 1873
28¼ x 36 in
Oil on canvas
Musée des Beaux-Arts, Pau

This modern portrait of men in their work environment was begun
when Degas visited his mother's family in New Orleans; it depicts
the male members of the family working in the cotton trade.
Despite France's rapid transition to modern capitalism, it was
generally felt that commerce and money-making was beneath
the high purposes of art. Degas was one of the very few artists to
paint such scenes – perhaps because his own social status
derived from his family's business activities. The steeply angled
floor enables Degas to depict men absorbed in different aspects
of commerce (the only ones not working are Degas's brothers).
Everyone is absorbed in his own activity, isolated from one
another by the linear framework created by windows, doors,
desks, and shelves. However, Degas creates formal unity
between the figures through his use of subtle scales of cream,
ochre, brown, and black paint, and thus suggests participation in
a collective enterprise, in purposive masculine mental activity.

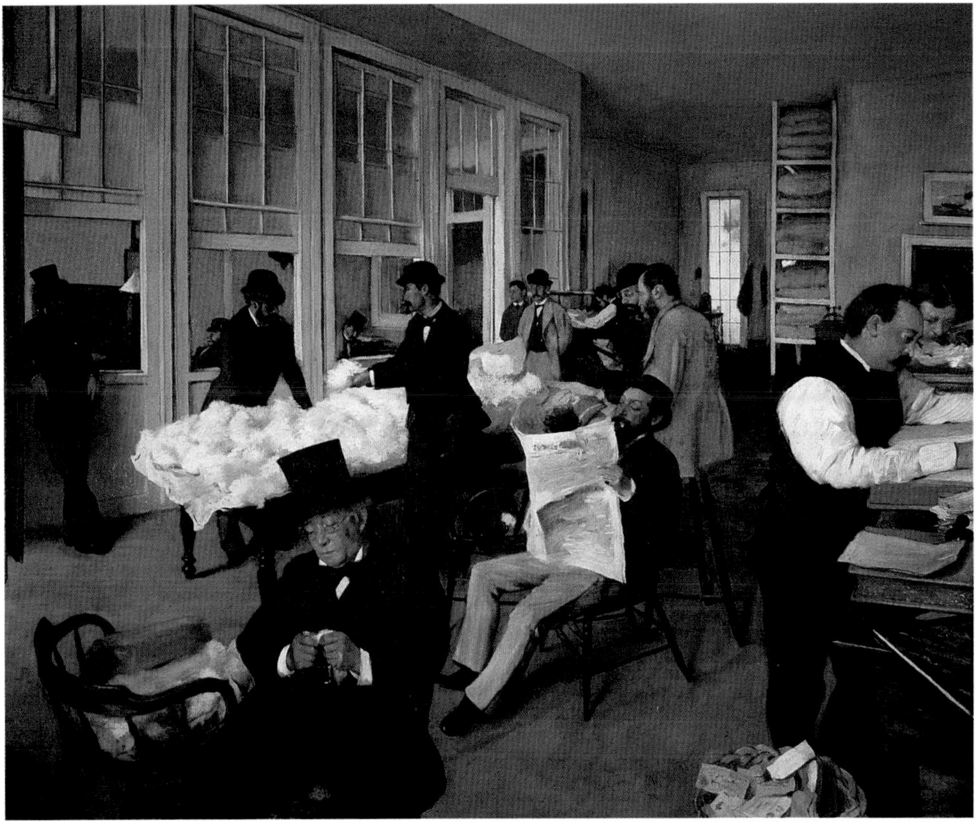

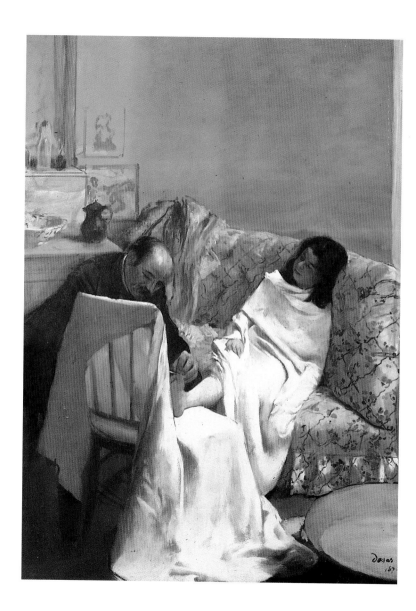

*The Pedicure* 1873
23¾ x 18 in
Oil on paper
Musée d'Orsay, Paris

It is impossible to know why Degas painted this unusual scene.
Given the rigid codes of gender of the nineteenth-century
bourgeoisie, one is surprised to see a man doing something
normally entrusted to a maid or nurse, just as one might wonder
at Degas's presence at the toilet of a young girl – who is thought
to have been his ten-year-old niece. This is the first example of
Degas's fascination with the grooming of women's bodies. Here,
the girl is swathed in white drapery, but in other respects – the
intimate interior, the details of toilet articles – the work is a
prefiguration of Degas's later images of women washing and
drying themselves (*see pages 107, 110, 120, 124, and 127*).

***The Rehearsal of the Ballet on Stage*** c.1874

20³/₄ x 28 in

Pastel over ink drawing

Metropolitan Museum of Art, New York

This, one of three versions of the same scene, again shows
the ballet dancers going through their endlessly rehearsed
movements. The scroll of the double-bass projects into the group
of dancers waiting to go on stage; one scratches her back, and
another yawns – instinctive physical actions that any respectable
woman would suppress. The dancers have low foreheads, puffy
cheeks, snub noses, and receding chins – all features that to the
upper classes were signs of the debased working-class woman.
Degas shared the attitudes of his class, but he did not dwell on
them. On stage, directed by the dance-master, the dancers are
transformed into momentary beauty. Degas may have seen the
ballet rehearsal as related to his own work as an artist, creating
something beautiful from crude, unformed materials, and doing
so by endless disciplined work in which every detail was scrutinized, weighed, and rehearsed.

***Dancer posing at a Photographer's*** 1875

25¼ x 19½ in

Oil on canvas

Pushkin Museum, Moscow

Much has been written about Degas's debt to photography. This painting suggests intersecting gazes: that of the photographer and that of the dancer, who examines her own image in the mirror, slightly squeezing her eyes to see from her tilted head. But Degas painted his work in the studio, from memory and from drawings of the pose in which he could explore different positions of the limbs. It was in the studio that he chose the scales of green, green-tinged whites, and a warmer pink-gold to suggest the glacial cold of the photographer's room and the buildings outside. For Degas, photography revealed unexpected ways of seeing – fragments, asymmetries – but he disliked what he felt was the passivity of the machine-eye, the camera. The painting insists on the painter's re-creation of external reality.

*Woman with Binoculars* 1875–76

18³/₄ x 12¹/₂ in

Oil on cardboard

Staatliche Kunstsammlungen, Dresden

Degas painted three studies of a woman staring out at the spectator through binoculars. The motif derives from a mid-1860s painting of a figure at a racecourse. Cassatt and Renoir also used binoculars or opera glasses to materialize the processes of looking. They force one to consider who was looking at whom and from what viewpoint. It was regarded as indecorous for a respectable woman to look fixedly at a man; the direct look could be that of a prostitute sizing up a client, but generally women were the object of the gaze. As one whose role was to look, Degas may have enjoyed the notion of reversing the roles and of being scrutinized by a woman assisted by the unnerving, insectlike gaze of the binoculars.

***Café-concert at the Ambassadeurs*** 1875–7

14½ x 10½ in

Monotype and pastel

Musée des Beaux-Arts, Lyons

Degas frequently painted working-class entertainments, including the *café-concert*, the French equivalent of the music-hall. Contemporary writers express the mixed disgust and excitement experienced by the upper classes when they went 'slumming' in such places: disgust at their proximity to the lower classes, to clerks, shop assistants, and prostitutes; excitement in the vitality so much at variance with their own rigid codes of correct behavior.

The work was executed in monotype – a print taken from an ink drawing and overlaid with vibrant strokes of pastel. Thus, although the work was executed in the studio, it suggests that Degas captured the moment when the singer, almost iridescent in the whiteness of gaslight, thrusts out her arm to her motley and degraded audience.

***Peasant Girls bathing in the Sea, Twilight*** 1875–6

25¼ x 31½ in

Oil on canvas

Private Collection

This painting is unique in Degas's work. At the end of his life he did paint several pictures on the traditional theme of women bathers in the open air, but none expresses the joys of the body as this work does. With wonderful economy, Degas evokes the chain of emotional movement from tentative entry into the water to ecstatic dance. It seems impossible that with such scratchy paint he could evoke the twilight shadow in the foreground and the almost visionary glimpse of the distant milky-white sea, the pink-and-white sky, and the orange of the setting sun. It is improbable that girls would swim naked on the heavily used beaches of northern France. Degas would have painted the work in the studio, probably using a nude model, and relying on vivid but fragmentary memories of the seascape.

***Sea-bathing: Little Girl having her Hair
combed by her Nurse*** *c.*1877

18¼ x 32¼ in

Oil on canvas

National Gallery, London

Degas showed both this beach scene and the *Peasant Girls
bathing in the Sea, Twilight* (*see page 65*) in the 1877
Impressionist exhibition. He very rarely depicted figures in
nature, preferring the artifice, even the corruption, of the city
(*see page 71*). The two paintings contrast the mythical freedom
of natural bodies with the constrained behavior of the urban
middle classes on holiday at the seaside. Wrapped in sheets, a
woman and the children emerging from the sea form a little
procession escorted by a maid. In the foreground, a nurse
almost tenderly combs the young girl's hair. The girl may have
been bathing, but nothing, except an ankle, is revealed of her
body. Her bathing costume is stretched out comically on the
sand, but there is little to link its abstraction to her subtly twisted
body.

A Painter of Modern Life

*Women on a Café Terrace, Evening* 1877

16 x 23½ in

Pastel on monotype

Musée d'Orsay, Paris

Degas represents prostitutes in a café that opens onto the
sinister glamour of a gas-lit boulevard, where they can display
their bodies like any other goods for sale in the modern society
of consumption. Even Degas later found this work 'rather cynical
and cruel.' His depiction of the women approaches caricature,
and embodies the middle-class view of the degenerate faces of
the urban working classes: two of the faces consist simply of a
nose and a disappearing chin. In describing such faces, writers
used the terms 'muzzle' or 'snout' – terms used to describe
animals. When it was shown in the 1877 Impressionist exhibition,
some critics thought Degas was intending to shock the
bourgeoisie; others saw it as a satire; another evoked the
'terrifying realism [of these] creatures, rouged, withered,
dripping with vice.'

***The Star,* or *Dancer on Stage*** 1876–7

22½ x 16½ in

Pastel on monotype

Musée d'Orsay, Paris

Degas shaped the dancer's body to give the impression that it
is spinning across space – at the moment it is caught by the
footlights. One leg, the upper part of the bust, the outstretched
arms, and the tilted head are enough to suggest the wholeness
of the body – indeed any more detail and the sense of turning
movement would be lost.

Her fluttering black ribbons lead the eye to the wings, from where
she is watched by a black-suited gentleman, a 'subscriber' who
had paid for the right to go back stage. Even partially seen, the
man seems to exert power across the space between himself
and the dancer. To modern eyes, the imbalance of power may
seem cruel; for Degas, it was simply a fact of life. Whatever the
case, the man's presence intensifies the poignancy of this
moment of beauty.

***Girl Dancer exercising at the Bar*** c.1878–80

12 x 9¼ in

Black chalk on paper

Fitzwilliam Museum, University of Cambridge

The witty brevity of this sketch of a skinny little girl also suggests that Degas's drawing could reveal sympathy for his subject. She takes up one of the standard ballet positions, turning her feet outwards and her head over her shoulder, and holding her arm parallel to her leg. But there is no sense that this little body has yet been 'broken into' the artificial pose, and the face suggests a childish weariness. Slight though it is, the drawing says much about the work that the child would have to undergo before she could hope to make a living as a dancer.

***The Racecourse: Amateur Jockeys near a Carriage*** c.1876–87

25³/₄ x 31¹/₂ in

Oil on canvas

Musée d'Orsay, Paris

Comparison between this painting and the *Carriage at the Races* (*see page 37*) shows that Degas's style had become broader and more abstract. The influence of Japanese prints is again strong, but the silhouettes of the carriage and the horses and their riders with their brightly colored silks are larger and more radically cut by the frame – so that the lady in the carriage is represented simply by her back and her grandiose hat, the gentleman by his arm, top hat, and a large ear. The flattened space allows Degas to express movement, not only through the horses' bodies, but also through the movement of the eye from left to right – a movement in which the dynamism of the steam train wittily prolongs and challenges that of the horse.

*Portrait of Edmond Duranty* 1879

39 x 39 in

Tempera and pastel

Glasgow Art Gallery and Museum, Glasgow

Degas seems to have known the Realist novelist and critic
Duranty since the mid-1860s, when they met with Manet, Zola,
and other painters and writers to argue over a new phase of
Realism – that dealing with modern urban life. A comment from
Duranty's brochure 'The New Painting' (1876) is relevant to this
portrait: 'What we need are the special characteristics of the
modern individual ... It is the study of the relationship of a man to
his home, or the particular influence of his profession on him, as
reflected in the gestures he makes; the observation of all aspects
of the environment in which he evolves and develops.'

*Portraits at the Stock Exchange* c.1878–9

39 x 32 in

Oil on canvas

Musée d'Orsay, Paris

This is another modern portrait of an individual in his
environment. It represents Ernest May, a rich financier and
art collector. Degas, who later became bitterly anti-Semitic,
shared the prejudices of his class against newly rich French
Jews. He depicted May on the steps of the Paris Stock
Exchange, heavily accentuating his nose and sallow complexion.
The dark suits, crowded to one side of the painting or crammed
behind a pillar; the shadowed or incomplete heads; the insistent
emphasis on hooked noses and the heavy gestures – all give the
painting a rather sinister character. It is, however, possible that
neither Degas nor May quite realized what the painting implies:
May accepted the work (even in its unfinished state);
it was shown in the 1880 Impressionist exhibition, and in 1923
May bequeathed it to the Louvre.

***Miss La La at the Fernande Circus*** 1879

45¾ x 30 in

Oil on canvas

National Gallery, London

The painting shows Miss La La, a mulatto acrobat, being
raised to the roof of the circus by a rope that she held in her
teeth. Her dark head is so rigidly drawn back that, without
seeing more, one can sense the immense strain on her body.
Degas expresses the tawdry glamour of the circus and of her
fashionably curvaceous body, as well as the excitement of her
ascent, by making pictorial use of the modern iron architecture –
which needs only slender supports to create soaring space – by
aligning her outstretched arm to the roof-rib, and her body to a
column, so that the eye sweeps upwards into the vault. But he
also reveals the mechanism of the moment of transcendence –
the taut rope that refuses any pictorial role and the touch of light
on the metal 'bit' between Miss La La's teeth.

*The Brothel* c.1879
5½ x 8 in
Monotype and pastel
Private Collection

Degas began his monotypes of brothel scenes in the late 1870s.
Realist novelists frequently wrote about the subject, but there is no
evidence that Degas ever exhibited any of his prints on this theme.
They are more a private exploration than an exposé directed at the
public. He expressed no judgements about what he depicts, but
obsessively probed the intimate life of the female body.

The monotype – which Degas called 'drawings done with
greasy ink and printed' – is an intimate technique: the prints
are usually tiny (less than 6 x 8 in), and sometimes the
marks of Degas's fingers smeared onto the plate can be seen
on them, as if conjuring the body to form. With his extraordinary
visual memory, he could, in the privacy of his studio, evoke
naked women lying on beds, embracing one another, washing
themselves. Sometimes he shows male clients looking them
over, or watching them while they washed. The male figures tend
to be puny or ridiculously rigid in the face of the women's vitality,
and it is possible to imagine Degas thinking of his own voyeurism
with a certain irony.

***At the Louvre: Mary Cassatt in the***
***Museum of Antiquities*** 1879–80
10½ x 9 in
Etching, aquatint, and electric crayon
Fitzwilliam Museum, University of Cambridge

Degas admired Mary Cassatt's paintings and maintained a long
friendship with her. Here he represents her contemplating an
Etruscan tomb-sculpture of a man and wife, while her sister
reads the catalog. Visiting museums and galleries together was
one activity outside the home open to middle-class women, but
here too, they had to display respectability – with their bodies
entirely swathed in clothes, and hair and hands concealed by
hats and gloves.

The implications of the confrontation between Cassatt and the
sculpture are ambiguous. If Degas meditated on the contrast
between the unmarried professional artist and the touching
representation of a marriage that transcends the death of the
couple, he gave no indication what he thought about it.

*The Little Dancer, aged 14* 1879–81

37 in high

Polychrome bronze with muslin, linen, and satin

(cast from the wax original after Degas's death)

Private Collection

Degas did many sculptures in wax, but this is the only one he exhibited. Degas tinted the wax so it resembled flesh, clothed the figure in silk, tulle, and gauze, gave it real hair and slippers, and, strangely, covered the bodice and slippers with a layer of wax. When it was shown in the 1881 Impressionist exhibition, the critic Huysmans claimed that it was 'the only truly modern attempt' in sculpture, and that its 'horrible realism' challenged a public used to the 'cold lifeless whiteness' of conventional sculpture.

What critics *saw* was shaped by the usual prejudices about dancers: the dancer was characterized as 'a precociously depraved flower … withered before her time,' and was seen as having a 'vicious muzzle' and forehead and lips 'marked … with a profoundly vicious character.' It is possible that, in a sculpture so like a figure in a waxworks, Degas was challenging himself: how close could he come to imitation and yet make a work of art? One critic was sure he had not succeeded: the sculpture, he said, should be put 'in a museum of zoology, anthropology, or physiology,' not in 'a museum of art.'

***Dancer adjusting her Tights*** *c*.1880–5

9¼ x 12 in

Black chalk, heightened with white, over pencil

Fitzwilliam Museum, University of Cambridge

Degas often depicted a seated dancer balancing on one leg
and stretching the other out before her. This drawing (squared
up for enlargement into a painting) shows the constant
adjustments he made to bodily form, not so much in search of
greater accuracy, but in order to express the dynamics of the
body. He wanted to express bodily sensations – here, for
example, the sensation of a leg tensed to support the body,
and counterpoising the stretch of the other leg. Anatomical
accuracy would have lessened these sensations.

***At the Theatre: Woman with Fan*** *c.*1880

27¼ x 18¼ in

Charcoal and pastel

Private Collection

This drawing is related to four pastels that make Degas's intense awareness of the ways in which sight is shaped by class and gender quite explicit. He depicts the viewpoint of someone with the wealth to hire or to visit a box at the Opéra, someone who is standing above the elegantly dressed lady seen here, looking down at and past her to the faintly depicted dancers on the stage below. She holds her fan in such a way that it would partially conceal her body from the audience, but one that allows the artist to look down on her body and on her low-cut evening dress. As if to emphasize that the composition is about sight, Degas stresses the silhouette of her other hand, which holds a pair of opera glasses. Simple though it is, the drawing suggests a network of gazes: that of the lady looking down on the dancers; that of the unseen audience to whom she displays herself; and that of the artist who can see everything.

***At the Milliner's*** 1882–6

39 x 43¼ in

Oil on canvas

Art Institute of Chicago

This is one of a group of works depicting milliners and their
clients produced between 1882 and 1886, most of which are in
pastel. Degas returned to the subject in the 1890s, and again in
the 1900s. They form part of that larger group of works in which
Degas depicts women caring for their bodies and preparing
themselves for appearance in public, as well as the women who
worked for them – maids, milliners, laundresses, and, on one
occasion, a seamstress. In some of the works, the clients are
accompanied by friends, making a visit to the milliner's a social
occasion. The ladies try on hats and scrutinize themselves in
mirrors; the milliners trim the hats, and hand them to the clients.
This painting shows a milliner absorbed in her task, but almost
dwarfed by the huge floral hats that she has helped to create.

***Scene in a Laundry*** 1884

24½ x 17½ in

Pastel

The Burrell Collection, Glasgow Museums and

Art Galleries, Glasgow


Laundresses were a favorite subject for graphic artists, who played on the general assumption that they were, like most working women, sexually promiscuous – a notion fostered by their economic vulnerability, and perhaps by the fact that they worked on the dirty linen of the middle classes. But Degas simply represents the exhaustion of bodies subject to constant hard, physical labor. The laundresses' work is spread along the table almost like an assembly line, curving past the slumped woman and the seated woman to the great pile of laundry on the floor; the wet washing hangs above in a translucent screen against the shop windows. This sense of endless process suggests that the seated woman is reading a laundry list, before returning to work. No one could have been less a social reformer than Degas, yet his depictions of laundresses almost convince one that he wanted to depict the truth of their condition – here, for example, the effects of hard work in humid, unhealthy rooms.

*Two Laundresses* 1884–86

29¾ x 31½ in

Oil on canvas

Musée d'Orsay, Paris


Degas did four versions of this composition. In this one, he used very dry paint on an unusually rough, unprepared canvas to give the image of hard, mundane labor something of the monumental simplicity of early Renaissance frescoes. He shows one woman in the throes of a huge yawn. Rigid standards of decorum would have prohibited middle-class women from displaying such instinctive bodily functions, let alone from being seen clutching a bottle of wine. Ironing was thirsty work, but the fact that laundresses sought to alleviate it with wine gave the upper classes another reason for considering them vulgar and promiscuous. But in his depiction of the hard, physical labor required to iron a voluminous starched shirt with a small iron (heated on the stove behind the woman), Degas emphasized these women's lives as workers, not as the sexualized figures of middle-class fantasy.

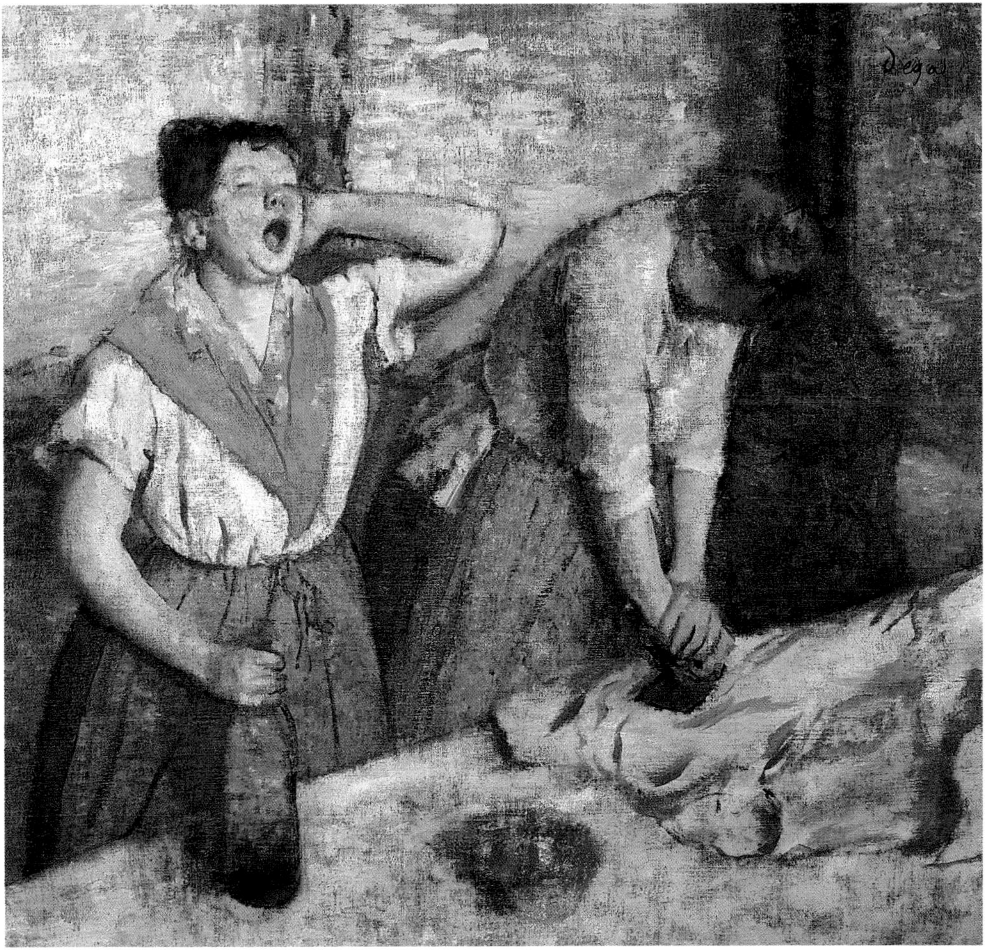

# Beyond Impressionism

WORKS BETWEEN 1886 AND 1910

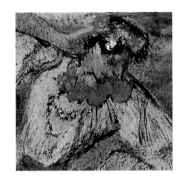

*The Bath* 1886
23½ x 32¼ in
Pastel
Musée d'Orsay, Paris

In the last Impressionist exhibition in 1886, Degas exhibited this work in a group of ten pastels called 'Series of female nudes bathing, washing, and drying themselves, combing their hair or having their hair combed' – a theme which he worked on throughout the 1880s and 1890s. It is a daring composition, with the crouched woman seen from above, her supporting arm stiff with her own weight, her curiously deformed right arm squeezing the sponge over her neck (two critics wrote of 'froglike' poses). The high viewpoint excludes any details of the interior, but allows Degas to lay out a water jug, brush, false hair, and a hand mirror – the intimate instruments of bodily grooming.

When these works were exhibited, some critics saw them as obscene representations of prostitutes. They admired the intensity of Degas's observation, but seem to have resented not his 'disdain for woman,' but his contempt for art. One claimed that Degas depicted not 'nudes,' but 'nakedness.' In other words, these were unclothed bodies that were not idealized according to conventional ideas of beauty which supposedly made the female nude asexual and therefore 'safe.'

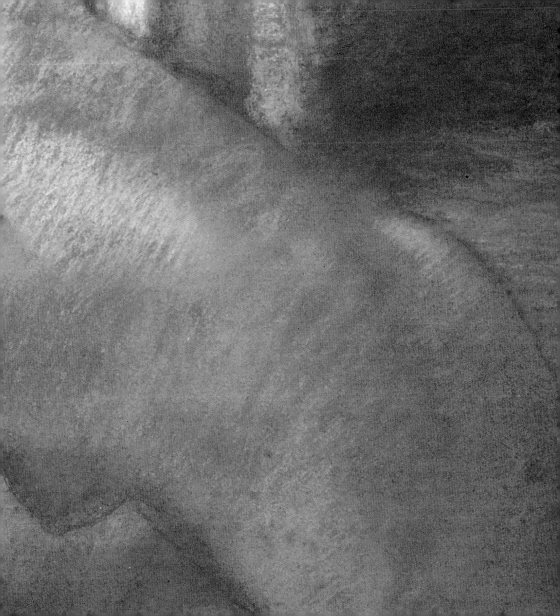

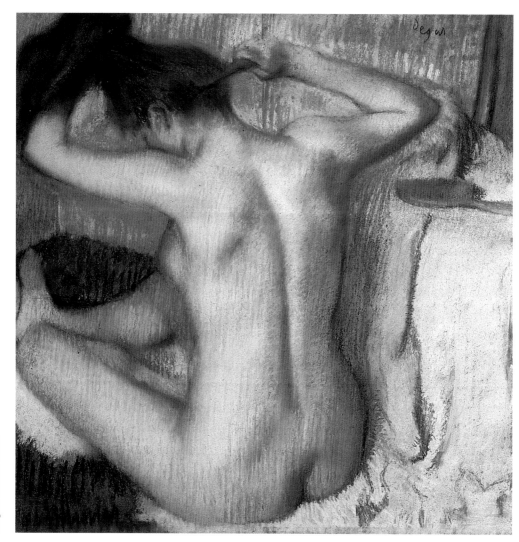

*Woman combing her Hair* c.1884–6

22¼ x 31¼ in

Pastel

Hermitage Museum, St Petersburg

Degas first tackled the subject of women washing and grooming themselves – his favored subject in the last two decades of his career – in his tiny brothel monotypes (*see page 86*). It is, however, strange that Degas, a great draftsman who had trained by drawing the nude, should have done so few nudes until the 1880s.

This pastel is one of the most classical of his nudes in its continuous contours and delicate modeling of luminous flesh. But the pose is anything but classical, for the woman is sitting with her legs askew and her right arm rigid, facing into the constricted corner of a room, seemingly unaware of being seen – unlike the classical nude who usually turns to the spectator. She is concentrating on untangling her long hair, and as one becomes aware of the stress on the arm pulling the hair tight, and the acute angle of the other, one comes to see the tension of the entire body. This is a body that is at work on that necessity of women's life, her self-presentation. Here, as elsewhere, Degas gives the impression that his model was completely absorbed in her own physicality.

### *Hélène Rouart in her Father's Study* c.1886

62¼ x 46¾ in

Oil on canvas

National Gallery, London

Hélène Rouart was the daughter of one of Degas's oldest friends, the wealthy industrialist Henri Rouart. Although she is posed quite informally, her body is completely unlike that of the yawning laundress (*see page 103*) in that it is shaped by decorum and the corset into the rigid forms of upper-middle-class propriety. There is poignancy in the contrast between the body and its small head with its slightly skewed features, and in the way she is almost imprisoned between the border of the Chinese wall-hanging, the sharp edges of the glass case, and the bars of her father's chair. As in other Degas's works, the chair signifies an absent person – here, Hélène's father.

The painting contains several works from Henri Rouart's collection: the rigidity of the Egyptian funerary sculptures makes Hélène's tentative stance more vulnerable, while Jean-Baptiste-Camille Corot's (1796–1875) luminous study of the Bay of Naples gives the only suggestion of a living world beyond this confined space. Degas's refusal to idealize the female figure once again gives the sense that his model has her own being – even if that is being defined by the patriarchal.

*Jockeys* 1886–90

Dimensions not known

Oil on canvas

Private Collection

By now, Degas's paintings of horses and riders had become like abstract friezes. The tilted plane of green grass and the dynamic silhouettes of the elegant horses and bright silks reveal his continuing interest in Japanese prints. In earlier paintings showing Japanese influence, such as *The Racecourse: Amateur Jockeys near a Carriage* (*see page 76*), the horses are drawn in full profile, whereas Degas now turns them quite sharply into depth, while still representing them as flat silhouettes. The contradiction between flatness and dynamic movement into depth gives great vitality to the work.

***Trotting Horse*** *c*.1888–90

8¹/₂ in high

Bronze

Private Collection


Degas did his first wax sculptures of horses in the late 1860s. They
are relatively static, but in his works of the late 1880s, he focused
on different forms of movement: trotting, rearing, cantering,
galloping, walking, etc. He was probably influenced by the photographic study of movement reproduced in Eadweard Muybridge's
*Animal Locomotion* in 1887 (and in the French journal *La Nature* in
1878). Photography could reveal aspects of movement not
previously seen, but Degas had been observing and depicting
movement for twenty years, and he knew that there was a
difference between the photographic 'freezing' of different phases
of movement and the pictorial or sculptural expression of dynamic
movement. He realized the latter in his paintings by fusing different
phases of movement in one animal (for instance, the horses in the
upper right of *Jockeys*; *see page 115*).

*Landscape* c.1890–2

19½ x 19½ in

Pastel

Museum of Fine Arts, Houston

Degas was scornful of his fellow Impressionist's practice of painting landscape in the open air, and he painted few pure landscapes, and then only at specific moments in his career. This is
one of a group of marvellously poetic landscapes executed in
monotype and pastel in the late 1880s and early 1890s. They
were all created from memory in the studio. There, he said, 'You
will reproduce only what has struck you, that is, what is essential.
There, your memory and your fantasy are liberated from the
tyranny of nature.' In this pastel, a breast-shaped rock and a
phallic rock are silhouetted against a huge plain with winding
rivers and hills tinted with roses and violets. As in other landscapes, the freeing of Degas's imagination led him to eroticize
nature in images that are sensuous and seductive, but which
also haunt one with their nagging sense of meaning that is just
beyond grasp.

***Woman combing her Hair*** *c*.1890–2

32 x 22¼ in

Pastel

Musée d'Orsay, Paris


Throughout his career, Degas had fears about his sight; by 1891 it was so bad that he found it difficult to read and write. This may partially explain the increasing scale of his figures, the breadth of his handling, and the simplification of colors into large areas of sumptuous richness. A woman combing her immensely long hair was one of his favored themes; here, its rich chestnut prolongs the colors of material above her head and pours across the surface in sweeping lines, so that her body is reduced to the angle of her breast, a fragment of the shadowed torso, arms, and a hint of a nose. For Degas the essential was the slow, self-absorbed, almost hypnotizing combing of the hair.

***Breakfast after the Bath*** 1895

47$\frac{1}{4}$ x 36 in

Pastel

Private Collection

The sumptuous colors of this interior glow in the filtered light that falls sensuously on the woman's body. She stands in an ungainly pose, with all her energy focused on drying her neck while she also holds up her hair, which cascades into the shadows of the curtains, where the towel flicks forward in a electric energy of intense blues and violets. The woman's body almost disintegrates in the long stabbing colored lines of pastel.

The arrival of the servant with the coffee introduces a note of ordinariness into the scene. It reminds one of the way in which Degas's work and life now interacted. One of his women friends criticized the fact that he kept toilet things, including a bath, in his 'gallery.' Degas replied that it was useful and that he bathed in it in the mornings. But it was also here that Degas asked his models to move freely until they took up a pose that attracted him. This suggests a life that had become absorbed by the processes of making art.

***Woman drying Herself*** 1896

30 x 37¾ in

Oil on canvas

Private Collection

Degas painted three versions of this strained pose, in which
the woman twists her body almost as if in an erotic spasm. He
shortened the lower leg, made the right arm almost stunted,
and once again reduced the head to little more than a support
for a cascade of hair. Nothing therefore interferes with the long
sinuous back and the sharp jut of legs and arm. Strangely, the
female body is reduced to a directional energy, while, on either
side of her, the curves of bath, jug, bowl, and sponge take on the
more common associations of the female body as container:
curvaceous, pink, soft, suggestive of unseen inner depths.

***Combing the Hair*** c.1896
48¼ x 58½ in
Oil on canvas
National Gallery, London

Degas composed this painting with a daringly simplified range of colors: a scale of reds, ranging from crimsons to brilliant orange; a lighter scale runs from the white tablecloth through the apron and blouse of the maid; these are accented by the yellow hairbrush, mirror, and comb and by stark purplish-blacks. The strangely threatening red space and simple expressive shapes make the reclining figure seem tense and even anguished. Unlike the measured actions of the women who comb their own hair, the maid's combing suggests something painful – as is indicated by the helpless arms, the drawn-back head, the slits of mouth, nostril and brows, and the coarse lines indicating the bulge and the stretch of the pregnant body. Degas's radical simplifications of color, space, and form look forward to the twentieth century – above all to Matisse's paintings of women in interiors.

***In the Wings (Dancers in Blue)*** *c.*1898

25¾ x 26¼ in

Pastel

Pushkin Museum, Moscow


In 1886 Degas had written, 'one must do the same subject over
again, ten times, a hundred times. Nothing in art must appear
accidental, not even a movement.' He had depicted dancers in
the wings since the early 1870s. In the *Rehearsal of the Ballet on
Stage* (*see page 55*), one can see variants of the poses used in
this late pastel: the dancer with her arm stretched against the
scenery; one adjusting her clothing; another bending to adjust
her shoe. In the later work, the dancers are less individualized,
and they suggest the essence of a group of women preparing
to appear before an audience rather than a specific scene.
The stagelights gleam on elbows or shoulders, bathing the
intense blues in an unearthly light. There are three photographs
thought to have been taken by Degas that show the dancer with
outstretched arm, and another showing her adjusting her dress.
They reduce the body even more radically to head, shoulders,
jutting arms only tenuously attached to bodies, and a shimmer
of fabric. In the pastel, Degas's emphatic lines and smears of
color show that these bodies are no more real than the
painted scenery.

## Group of Dancers *c*.1898

18 x 23¾ in

Oil on canvas

National Gallery of Scotland, Edinburgh

Degas had done earlier versions of this group, but repetition now seems less a matter of the artist's perfecting form than of his obsessively feeling his way into what is essential in these bodies. For example, the central figure consists essentially of a chin, a gracefully turned neck and shoulder, a triangular torso with a pulled-in waist, a skirt, two arms, and two legs. These few remains of the body suggest that the old, partially sighted man was painting only those parts of the dancer that conveyed bodily tension, almost as if he was imagining himself into the dancer's sensation of the turn in her neck and the upper body, or the stress on her ankle and the arch of her foot. The skirts no longer suggest tulle and muslin but are emphatically layers of colored pastes – pinks, whites, mauves, greens – with broken lines that hint at the directional movement of the bodies. A mirror reflecting part of the skirt and a veiled window recall all those mirrors reflecting dancers that Degas had painted. Perhaps, too, the emerald green smeared over warmer colors responds to memory of cold gaslight.

***Russian Dancers*** 1899

$24^1/_4$ x $24^1/_2$ in

Pastel

Museum of Fine Arts, Houston

Degas clearly appreciated the flat-footed, earth-based dances of the Russians. Their bodies contrast dramatically with his depictions of ballet dancers poised on the surface of floors, seemingly just brushing them with their delicate slippers, or touching them with the tips of their toes. Degas tended to ignore ballerinas' upper legs, which disappear under layers of tulle, but he emphasized the Russian dancers' knees and thighs and thus creates dynamic movement and strong, exhilarating rhythms. With flowers in their long hair and swinging skirts of brilliant color, the Russian dancers suggest something primitive and closer to nature than the refined artifice of their Parisian counterparts.

**Dancer looking at the Sole of her Right Foot** c.1895–1910

18½ in high

Bronze

Private Collection

After his death, Degas's many wax sculptures were found in his studio in a dilapidated condition; those not too damaged were afterwards cast in bronze. He seems to have begun his sculptures of dancers only in the 1880s (*see page 90*). He never exhibited any of his sculptures of the nude, so they were probably yet another form of private experimentation – and one that became particularly important when his increasing blindness drew him towards an art based on touch as much as sight. This is the latest of four versions of the same pose – which is closer to the twisted figures of his bathers than to any ballet position (these works were titled posthumously). One of his models described how she had to balance on one leg, pull her foot high, twist her head and upper body to see her sole, and counterbalance the backwards movement with her raised left arm. Degas constructs the body so as to give the impression of the momentariness of the pose.

***At the Milliner's*** 1905–10

35½ x 29¼ in

Pastel

Musée d'Orsay, Paris

This is one of Degas's last works before he went blind. It, too, returns to an earlier subject (*see page 97*), but one that is now expressed in large flat areas of color and simple silhouettes from which all individuality has been erased. The knotted hands of the servant are the most defined forms. They recall Degas's comment that what he enjoyed most when he accompanied a lady to a dress-fitting was the 'red hands of the little girl who holds the pins.' His works depict the infinity of actions that went into the presentation of women: their own hands washing, combing, adjusting ribbons, tights, and shoes; the hands of servants combing hair, ironing clothes, making hats. Without the outstretched hand of the servant, the pastel would not suggest the endless processes of manual labor. But it was the artist's hands that had conjured this world into being.

# Chronology

| | |
|---|---|
| **1834** | Born 19 July, in Paris, the eldest son of Auguste and Marie Célestine De Gas |
| **1855** | Enrols in the École des Beaux-Arts, as a pupil of Louis Lamothe, a follower of Ingres |
| **1856–9** | Studies independently in Italy |
| **1862** | Meets Manet while copying in the Louvre |
| **1866-8** | First exhibit at the Salon: *War-scene from the Middle Ages,* his last history painting |
| **1870–1** | During the Siege of Paris enrols in the National Guard, but leaves Paris during the Commune |
| **1872** | First paintings of dancers rehearsing; visits his mother's family in New Orleans; his eyes are already too weak to paint outdoors in brilliant light |
| **1873** | First transactions in Paris with Paul Durand-Ruel |
| **1874** | Left in financial difficulties by father's death; shows ten pictures at the first Impressionist bition |
| **1876–81** | Exhibits at the next five Impressionist exhibi |
| **1882** | Disputes with other Impressionists lead to c sion not to exhibit at the seventh Impression exhibition |
| **1883** | Exhibits in London |
| **1886** | Exhibits 15 works at the eighth, and last, Impressionist exhibition |
| **1891** | Solo exhibition of landscape monotypes at Galerie Durand-Ruel |
| **1891–6** | Broadens his style due to worsening eyesig |
| **1912** | Now blind, he probably ceases all work |
| **1917** | 27 September: death of Degas |

# Sources and Further Reading

Carol Armstrong, *Odd Man Out: Readings of the Work and Reputation of Edgar Degas*, Chicago and London, 1991

Richard Kendall, *Degas Landscapes*, New Haven and London, 1993

Richard Kendall and Griselda Pollock (eds), *Dealing with Degas: Representations of Women and the Politics of Vision*, London, 1992

Henri Loyrette, *Degas*, exh. cat., Grand Palais, Paris, and Metropolitan Museum of Art, New York, 1988

# Index